anythink

D0895646

5 STEPS TO DRAWING
SEA CREATURES

by Amanda StJohn • illustrated by Laura Ferraro Close

The Child's World

Published by The Child's World®
1980 Lookout Drive • Mankato, MN 56003-1705
800-599-READ • www.childsworld.com

ACKNOWLEDGMENTS
The Child's World®: Mary Berendes, Publishing Director
The Design Lab: Design and production
Red Line Editorial: Editorial direction

ISBN: 978-1-60973-204-2
LCCN: 2011927713

Printed in the United States of America
Mankato, MN
July 2011
PA02088

TABLE OF CONTENTS

SKIN AND SCALES

Fish have been around for about 500 million years. They were swimming in seas even before dinosaurs walked on Earth.

Most fish have scales. Scales are thin, bony plates that protect a fish's skin. A fish's skin can be very colorful. A clown fish has bright orange skin. Fish scales are almost see-through. They do not give a fish its color.

Some scales grow as a fish gets older to help cover its bigger body. Other scales never grow larger. New scales grow to cover up the growing body. Scales come in several shapes and sizes. They can be diamonds, rectangles, or ovals. Shark and ray scales are very tiny. They make these creatures look smooth. Koi fish have very large scales. Some koi scales are shaped like kernels of corn.

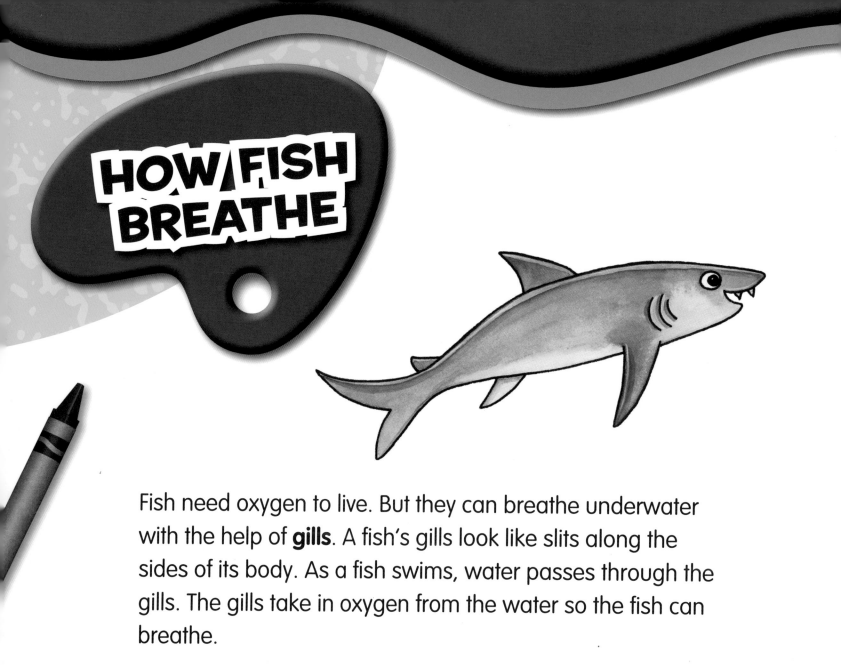

HOW FISH BREATHE

Fish need oxygen to live. But they can breathe underwater with the help of **gills**. A fish's gills look like slits along the sides of its body. As a fish swims, water passes through the gills. The gills take in oxygen from the water so the fish can breathe.

Inside the fish's gills are tiny, thin **tissues**. In the water, these tissues can float freely. This is just like how your hair spreads out on its own in the bathtub. But, if you take a fish out of the water, these tissues get heavy and stick together. This is like how your hair falls flat when you get out of the tub. If the gill tissues stick together, the fish cannot breathe. That is why fish need to be in water to stay alive.

OTHER SEA CREATURES

Sea creatures other than fish live in the water, too. But some, like sea turtles and orcas, cannot breathe underwater. They need oxygen from the air. They must come above water to breathe. They hold their breath and dive back underwater. Active orcas may take a breath every three minutes. Some sea turtles can sleep underwater for several hours.

Lobsters are another type of sea creature. They are part of an animal family called crustaceans. Like an insect, a crustacean has a very soft body. A hard shell protects the soft body. This shell is called an **exoskeleton**.

Another type of sea creature is a cephalopod. One kind of cephalopod is the giant squid. The giant squid has many tentacles, or arms.

DRAWING TIPS

You've learned about sea creatures. You're almost ready to draw them. But first, here are a few drawing tips:

Every artist needs tools. To learn how to draw sea creatures, you will need:

- Some paper
- A pencil
- An eraser
- Markers, crayons, colored pencils, or watercolors (optional)

Anyone can learn to draw. You might think only some people can draw. That's not true. Everyone can learn to draw. It takes practice, though. The more you draw, the better you will be. With practice, you will become a true artist!

Everyone makes mistakes. This is okay! Mistakes help you learn. They help you know what not to do next time. Mistakes can even make your drawing more special. It's all right if you draw the fish's fins too big. Now you've got a one-of-a-kind drawing. You can erase a mistake you don't like, too. Then start again!

Stay loose. Relax your body before you begin. Hold your pencil lightly. Don't rest your wrist on the table. Instead, move your whole arm as you draw. This will help you make smooth lines. Press lightly on the paper when you draw or erase.

Drawing is fun! The most important thing about drawing is to have fun. Be creative. They don't have to look exactly like the pictures in this book. Try changing the size of the scales. You can also use markers, crayons, colored pencils, or watercolors to bring your sea creatures to life.

1

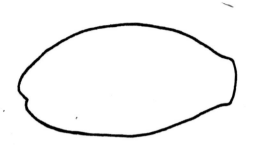

2

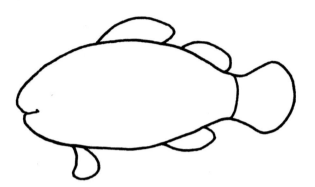

CLOWN FISH

3

4

If you see two clown fish together, the larger one is a female. Clown fish are covered in mucus. This protects them from being poisoned by the **sea anemones** they live among.

5

1

2

GREAT WHITE SHARK

3

4

Great white shark teeth are lined up in several rows. If they break a tooth off while eating, a tooth from the next row will move forward and take its place.

1

2

ORCA

3

4

16

An orca is also called a killer whale. On an orca's back is a gray patch of color. This shape is different on each orca. It acts like a name tag for scientists.

5

1

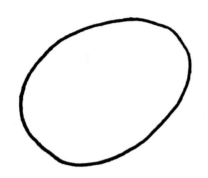

2

SEA TURTLE

3

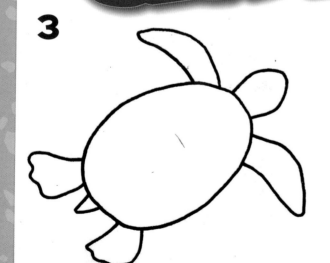

4

18

Sea turtles cannot hide inside their shells. Their shells have **scutes**. These are the things that look like scales. The number of scutes on a sea turtle's shell can tell you what kind of sea turtle it is.

1

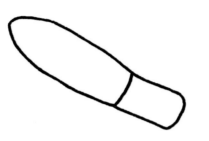

2

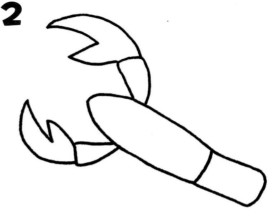

LOBSTER

3

4

A lobster's claws do not look the same. The crusher claw is very large and used for crushing things. The pincher claw is smaller. It is better for quickly grabbing things.

5

1

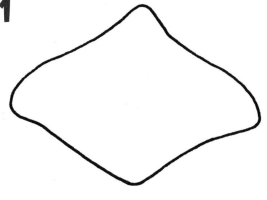

2

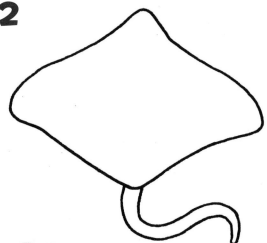

RAY

3

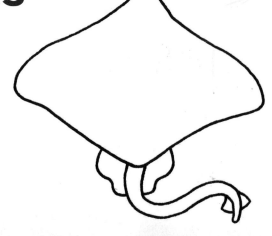

4

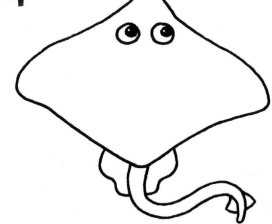

22

Rays are related to sharks. They are much flatter, though. Most rays move slowly. Their mouths and gills are on their bellies. They feed on the bottoms of oceans.

5

1

2

GIANT SQUID

3

4

The eyes of a giant squid are the size of basketballs. This squid swims backward and forward. It sprays ink when in danger.

5

1

2

SEAHORSE

3

4

26

A seahorse's tail is **prehensile**. This means it can clasp things by wrapping around them. The tail can grab hold of sea plants. Then the seahorse will not be swept away in a strong current.

5

MORE DRAWING

Now you know how to draw sea creatures. Here are some ways to keep drawing them.

Sea creatures come in all different colors, shapes, sizes, and textures. You can draw them all! Try using pens or colored pencils to draw and color in details. Experiment with crayons and markers to give your drawings different colors and textures. You can also paint your drawings. Watercolors are easy to use. If you make a mistake, you can wipe it away with a damp cloth. Try tracing the outline of your drawing with a crayon or a marker. Then paint over it with watercolor. What happens?

Drawing Real Sea Creatures

When you want something new to draw, take a field trip. Visit a zoo or an aquarium. Find a sea creature you want to draw. First, look at your sea creature carefully. Is it big or small? Does it have big or small scales? Does it need to be in water? Now try drawing it! If you need help, use the examples in this book to guide you.

GLOSSARY

exoskeleton (eks-oh-SKEL-ut-un): An exoskeleton is the bony structure on the outside of an animal. A lobster has an exoskeleton.

gills (GILS): Gills are body organs that a fish breathes through. Gills are on the side of a fish's body.

prehensile (pree-HEN-sul): If something is prehensile, it can be used to grab or hold objects. Seahorses have prehensile tails.

scutes (SKOOTS): Scutes are bony plates. A sea turtle has scutes on its shell.

sea anemones (SEE uh-NEM-uh-nees): Sea anemones are marine animals that look like flowers. Clown fish live among sea anemones.

tissues (TISH-oos): Tissues are groups of similar cells that form a part of an animal or a plant. A fish's gills have tissues that help the gills work in water.

FIND OUT MORE

BOOKS

Emberley, Ed. *Ed Emberley's Drawing Book: Make a World*. New York: Little Brown, 2006.

Levin, Freddie. *1-2-3 Draw Ocean Life*. Columbus, NC: Peel Productions, 2005.

Masiello, Ralph. *Ralph Masiello's Ocean Drawing Book*. Watertown, MA: Charlesbridge, 2006.

WEB SITES

Visit our Web site for links about drawing sea creatures:

childsworld.com/links

Note to Parents, Teachers, and Librarians: We routinely verify our Web links to make sure they are safe and active sites. So encourage your readers to check them out!

INDEX

ABOUT THE AUTHOR:
Amanda StJohn is a poet and children's book author from Toledo, Ohio. She and her father enjoy fishing for walleye on Lake Erie.

ABOUT THE ILLUSTRATOR:
For the last 25 years, Laura Ferraro Close has been illustrating children's books. She lives in Massachusetts with her husband, two sons, and dog. For her illustrations, Laura used a waterproof ink pen and watercolors that come in tubes.